This is a gift to:

Message:

From:

Date:

*Anchors of Hope*

Published by Christian Art Publishers,
PO Box 1599, Vereeniging, 1930, RSA

© 2014

First edition 2014

Designed by Christian Art Publishers
Images used under license from Shutterstock.com

Scripture quotations are taken from the *Holy Bible*, New International Version® NIV®. Copyright © 1973, 1978, 1984, 2011 by International Bible Society. Used by permission of Biblica, Inc.® All rights reserved worldwide.

Scripture quotations are taken from the *Holy Bible*, New Living Translation®. Copyright © 1996, 2004, 2007 by Tyndale House Foundation. Used by permission of Tyndale House Publishers Inc., Carol Stream, Illinois 60188. All rights reserved.

Scripture quotations are taken from the New King James Version. Copyright © 1979, 1980, 1982 by Thomas Nelson, Inc. Used by permission. All rights reserved.

Printed in China

ISBN 978-1-4321-0975-2

© All rights reserved. No part of this book may be reproduced in any form without permission in writing from the publisher, except in the case of brief quotations in critical articles or reviews.

15  16  17  18  19  20  21  22  23  24  –  11  10  9  8  7  6  5  4  3  2

# ANCHORS of HOPE

CHRISTIAN ART PUBLISHERS

It's tough to endure when the going is **rough,** but conquest awaits those whose heart is **tough.**

God didn't promise us sailing without a storm, but peace of heart amidst the storm and a safe landing if we entrust the seamanship to Him.

**Blessed** is the one who perseveres under trial. James 1:12

When in deep waters, tell yourself, "My head I'll keep up, for I'm not going under, I'm going through," and keep on swimming.

The manner in which we face storms from the outside depends on the **faith in God** we have on the inside.

If you want to enjoy the scenery from the crest of the mountain, you have to do the climbing.

When facing utmost strife
and on the stormy sea of life
you're drifting and feeling lost
by the waves you're beaten
and tempest tossed.
Of this you have to be sure:
to prevail you have to endure.
But the only one to impede you
from living a life of unrivaled victory,
rather than surrendering to mediocrity;
**he is the one called you!**

**Success** is not luck. It's hard work, determination, and endurance.

May He give you the

*desire of*

*your*

*heart*

and make all your plans succeed.

Ps. 20:4

Be prepared to meet the challenges *of life* and to endure failure — it's part of the winning game.

With God in your life you don't have to despair when storms of life as dark as night abound. People say, "Where there is life, there is hope," but God says, "Where I am, darkness turns into light."

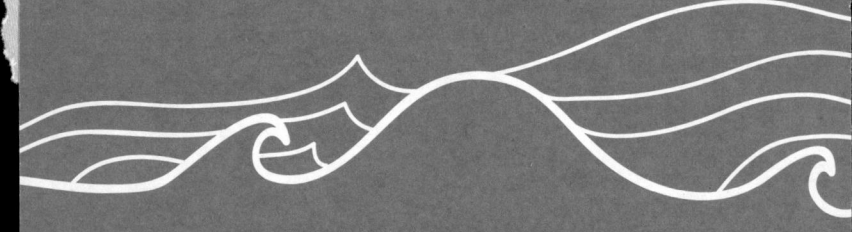

**Hope in your heart
is a hurricane lantern
in a stormy night.**

Unattainable goals become achievable goals by building on the foundation of faith in God, using the bricks of "I can" and the mortar of endurance.

**Faith,** courage, determination and **endurance** inconceivable are the wheels of the vehicle to mount to heights unbelievable.

**Faith is being sure of what we hope for and certain of what we do not see.**

**Heb. 11:1**

**Keep on doing the right thing right and it will become a habit.**

Make a habit of doing
for others
as you would like them
to do for you.

"Give, and it will be given to you. A good measure, pressed down, shaken together and running over."

**Luke 6:38**

It's easier giving up *good habits* than bad ones.

It only takes a decision to give up a good habit. It takes determination and perseverance to let go of bad habits. But the difference between the two is the hallmark of distinction between

## a winner

and a loser.

Changing habits without changing your heart is like trying to catch day and night in the same cup.

Make a habit of being considerate of people who have opinions that differ from yours, and listen without disparagement. Not only is it displaying respect; you may find something worthwhile to learn as well.

What does the Lord require of you? To act justly and to **love mercy** and to walk humbly with your God.

Mic. 6:8

Do not let any unwholesome talk come out of your mouths, but only what is helpful for building others up according to their needs, that it may benefit those who listen.

Eph. 4:29

a relationship
is like an investment:
If you don't care for it,
you'll lose interest and
eventually go bankrupt.

If all "if only's … could be buried, the world would not be big enough for the graveyard.

**Remember that the Lord will reward each one of us for the *good* we do.**

Eph. 6:8

**By kindling a fire**

**for someone else**

**you also**

**warm yourself.**

**Prosperity is the boon of hard work; poverty is the gloom of laziness.**

"Seek the Kingdom of God above all else, and live righteously, and He will give you everything you need."

Matt. 6:33

If you are shaken by storms in your life and doubt clouds your mind, stand your ground by having **unwavering faith** founded on the rock of God's promises that give you hope.

When life's tempest around you is raging and billows of waves are tossing high, God will unremittingly **care for you** as you trust Him more and more.

# Seized opportunities are the seeds of a rich harvest.

A man who

prides himself much

is prized little.

Where there is strife,

there is pride,

but **wisdom**

is found in those

who take advice.

Prov. 13:10

**Bad decisions result from bad thinking.**

Laziness empties the barn; diligence keeps from harm.

**Because of laziness the building decays, and through idleness of hands the house leaks.**

Eccles. 10:18

We are free to *believe* what we choose, but we cannot escape eating the fruit of what we choose to believe.

A great deal of satisfaction can be gained from any job, however difficult or boring it may be, by doing it to the best of your ability and with *enthusiasm.*

**You forfeit the ability to reign over problems by allowing the**

rain of the storms of life to drown your faith in God.

**Enthusiasm is to people what the wind is to a boat's sail – it moves them forward if skillfully handled.**

Be of good courage, and He shall strengthen your heart, all you who hope in the Lord.

Ps. 31:24

a person

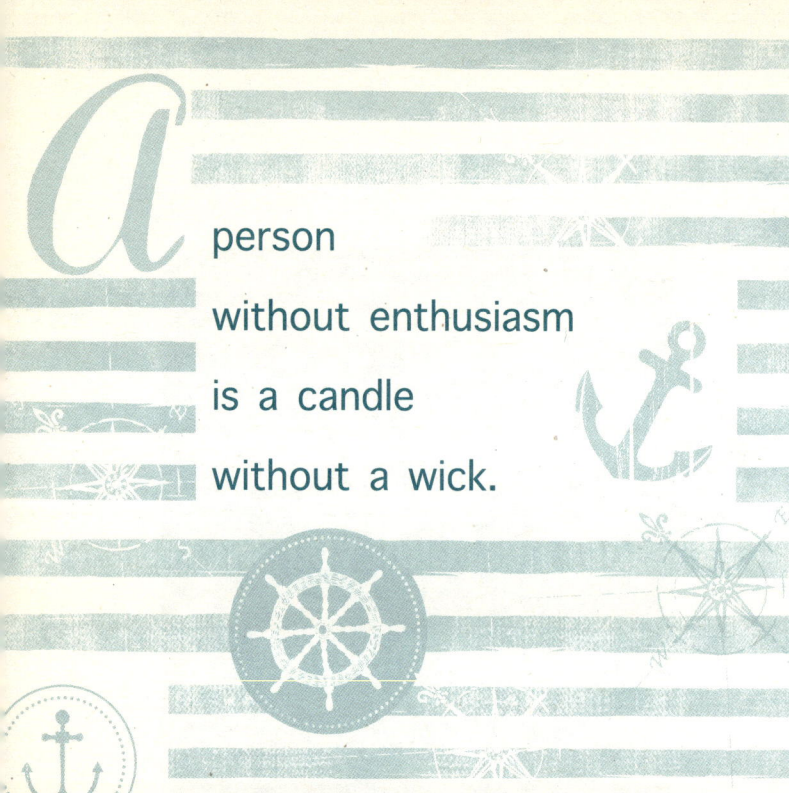

without enthusiasm

is a candle

without a wick.

*The greater the enthusiasm, the smaller the difficulties to overcome.*

# The joy of the Lord is your strength!

**Neh. 8:10**

Share your vision with **passion** and **enthusiasm** and others will be keen to follow.

**Enthusiasm,**
more than talent,
determines
quality of life.

The view from the crest of the mountain awaits only those who persistently press forward in spite of the strain of the climb.

**Don't allow the storms of life to sink your hopes and drown your dreams.**

Press forward against the wind of adversity. Just one more step may lead to **victory,** if you pin your hope on God and keep pressing on in spite of difficulty.

In a crisis be a skipper braving a stormy sea and likewise honing your skills for embarking on **greater challenges.**

**Take up your positions; stand firm and see the deliverance the Lord will give you.**

2 Chron. 20:17

Press forward
against the winds of adversity.
Without the *wind*
a kite cannot *soar.*

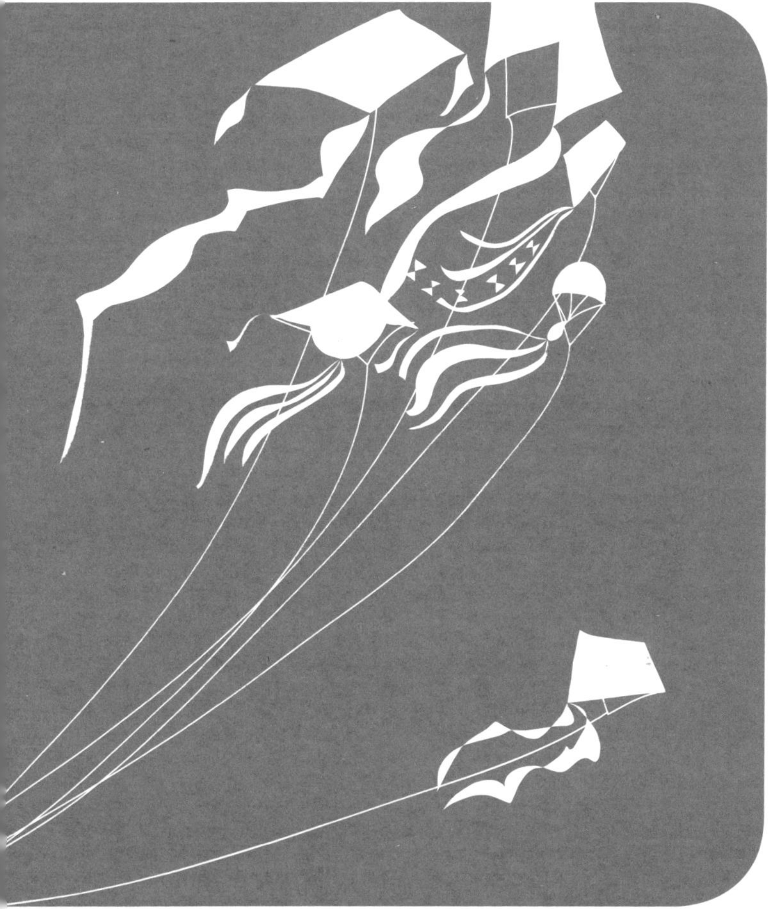

As plants grow towards the sun even in winter, we also have to move forward despite the hardships of life.

**Not the fear of challenges but the fear of failure has to be overcome before you can taste the fruit of victory.**

**All athletes are disciplined in their training. They do it to win a prize that will fade away, but we do it for an eternal prize.**

1 Cor. 9:25

You cannot manage the rough waters of life, but you can learn to ride the waves skillfully.

**Uncontrolled fear breaks the spirit of rulers.**

Fulfilling *your vision* is not plain sailing, but the delight of achievement pays for the voyage.

First you have to overcome the fear of hurt before you can make yourself heard in the world of pioneers.

A man with a vision is a skipper knowing his direction and reaching his destination even against the wind.

"I am the Lord your God who takes hold of your right hand and says to you, Do not fear; I will help you."

Isa. 41:13

Set your heart on serving others, and it will become a **treasure** for you that will never fade away.

To be **successful** you have to cross the abyss of the fear of failure.

For fear of failure,

substitute faith in God

in your vocabulary

and see how you rise

to incredible heights in

**victory.**

# Faith

in God is to set the sails of your lifeboat to reach your destination regardless of the direction of the wind.

"When you go through deep waters, I will be with you. When you go through rivers of difficulty, you will not drown. When you walk through the fire of oppression, you will not be burned up; the flames will not consume you. For I am the Lord, your God, *your Savior.*"

Isa. 43:2-3

Fear is the strongest
humanly created
prison bars;
the root of trees bearing
rotten fruit of doubt;
the nullifier of

**faith**

and the architect
of failure.

Feed your fears and you deplete **your strength and courage** to face adversity and conquer it unflinchingly.

"Don't be afraid; you are more valuable to God than a whole flock of sparrows."

Matt. 10:31

To live victoriously is not a matter of living without fear, but to conquer fear by accepting God's perfect gift *of love* towards us.

**Everything that was written in the past was written to teach us, so that through the endurance taught in the Scriptures and the encouragement they provide we might have hope.**

Rom. 15:4

The will to persevere marks *the difference* between progress and regress.

**Perseverance** is an extremely bitter experience many a time, but its fruit of **victory** is deliciously sweet all the time.

"This is My command — *be strong* and courageous! Do not be afraid or discouraged. For the Lord your God is with you wherever you go."

Josh. 1:9

If in the battles of life
you feel like quitting,
remember, it's in the heat
of the furnace that
God is in the process
of making
you a pillar of strength
in His service.

Quitters never win and **winners** never quit.

**Don't stop trying in trying times. It's the fisherman who continually casts his bait who takes home the fish.**

The Lord upholds

all those who fall

*and lifts up*

all who are

bowed down.

Ps. 145:14

When you've reached the end of your tether and you feel like sinking beneath the load, hang in there. When you're down to nothing, God is up to something!

If you've done all the standing you could and the wind of adversity roars against you, tell yourself, "By God's grace, I'll just stand."

When your **courage** is put to the test, hold on to your faith in God to turn your trials into triumphs.

Don't give up.
# Look up!
God knows each star by name.

He also knows your name and He

cares for you by day and by night.

We are pressed on
every side by troubles,
but we are not crushed.
We are perplexed,
but not driven to despair.
We are hunted down,
but never abandoned by God.
We get knocked down,
but we are not destroyed.

2 Cor. 4:8-9

*Sailing in calm waters*
all the time leads to a landing
in comfort zones
on a shore of mediocrity.

God did not promise a life without trials, but to give us **strength** to endure and **peace** amidst the storm.

If the pioneers who revolutionized technology stopped before the "*impossible*" you wouldn't be reading this.

**Remember,
when things go wrong
and your hopes and
dreams are falling apart,
God is there, He'll give you
a fresh start.
In your life He'll work
a revival,**

'cause to Him failure is not final.

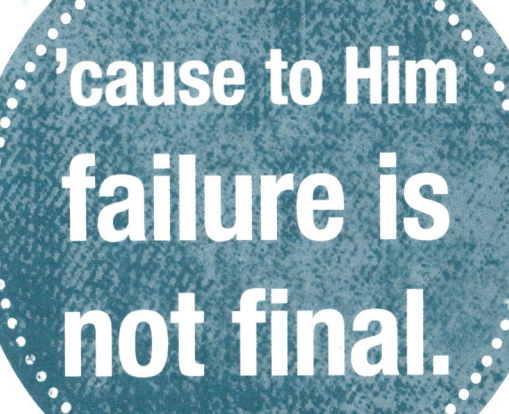

> **Let us not become weary in doing good, for at the proper time we will reap a harvest if we do not give up.**
>
> Gal. 6:9

# Don't quit!

You'll never know how close to victory you are. One more try may lead to triumph. Therefore, **just don't quit!**

# Patient endurance

is what you need now, so that you will continue to do God's will. Then you will receive all that He has promised.

Heb. 10:36

**Don't try to move a pile of rocks at once – do it by persistently carrying away one rock at a time, day after day.**

Never give up on yourself.
God has not;
neither does He intend
giving up on you!

**By refreshing others you are refreshing yourself.**

**By giving** **you are receiving.**

**The generous will prosper; those who refresh others will themselves be refreshed.**

Prov. 11:25

**Greatness in God's eyes is not measured by what we have become, but by the way we serve Him and others in a spirit of humility.**

True **humility** and the fear of the Lord lead to riches, honor, and long life.

Prov. 22:4

It's not how much you benefit from life, but how beneficial your life has been to others **that really matters** in the end.

"I have raised you up for this very purpose, that I might show you My power and that My name might be proclaimed in all the earth."

Exod. 9:16

**Encouragement**
incubated in a kind
heart is borne on
a heartened tongue.

A word of
# *encouragement*
may be the turning point of
a burdened life into a blooming life.

The gift of *encouragement* is to keep someone on his feet who, if left to himself, would collapse.

**Encourage** each other and build each other up.

1 Thess. 5:11

# Love

one another deeply,
from the heart.

1 Pet. 1:22

Be gentle with others. They are each rowing their own boat in a stormy sea.